How to Win at Penny Stocks

How to Win at Penny Stocks

Inside The Insiders

Jerry Greene

Copyright © 2012 by Jerry Greene.

ISBN: Softcover   978-1-4691-3748-3
          Ebook   978-1-4691-3749-0

All rights reserved. No part of this book may be reproduced or transmitted in any form or by any means, electronic or mechanical, including photocopying, recording, or by any information storage and retrieval system, without permission in writing from the copyright owner.

This book was printed in the United States of America.

To order additional copies of this book, contact:
Xlibris Corporation
1-888-795-4274
www.Xlibris.com
Orders@Xlibris.com
74500

> DISCLAIMER: Buying and selling stocks is gambling. No amount of advice or tips or strategies, including the information presented here for consideration only, is a guarantee of anything other than you may win or you may lose.

HOW TO WIN AT PENNY STOCKS—A Strategy

I was once watching TV late at night and a 'paid advertising' show came on. The advertiser was trying to sell his book or method on winning at stocks, and the announcer was acting like an impartial emcee, e.g. "So tell us how your incredibly successful stock bidding strategy is? Is it really so easy someone with no experience in the stock market can use it?"

The author who was being 'interviewed' then began an explanation for how his incredibly easy win method worked that went essentially like this:

AUTHOR: Let's take a look at this stock chart. Now notice here the value is at $1 per share. Let's watch it as it climbs to $1.20 per share. Do you see the peak here at $1.20?

ANNOUNCER: Yes.

AUTHOR: Now this is where many people would consider selling. Let's watch now as the stock drops back to $1.10 per share. Do you see here that the stock is now only worth $1.10 per share?

ANNOUNCER: Yes, I see that.

AUTHOR: Now let's watch the stock as it starts to rise again, here it is back at $1.20, and now $1.30 and finally at $1.50. Do you see that?

ANNOUNCER: Yes, I do.

AUTHOR: Here is where I sell the stock, at $1.50, making 30% more profit than the people who chose to sell it at $1.20.

ANNOUNCER: That is amazing. People who chose to sell at the $1.20 peak would of only made a 20% profit, but people who followed your method and waited until the stock hit $1.50 would have made a 50% profit. It seems so obvious and simple.

AUTHOR: It is, and my book will guide you through the process of buying and selling at the right time. Anyone can use this method.

Oh well, the average intellect of people that watch paid advertising shows is probably not that high; likely many viewers bought into the "If you buy low and sell high, you can make money in stocks" incredibly easy winning solution.

However, penny stocks, typically those announced by the 'major' penny stock announcement companies, tend to show a pattern that is more dependent on a predictable pattern of manipulation than the unpredictable pattern of a company's success, new products, market mobility, or whatever insider tips are happening behind closed doors. Once the announcement arrives in your email, in this case from one of the 'major' penny stock promotion companies, a roller coaster ride begins with losses and gains vastly exceeding what would happen with a 'real' company. Whether or not these penny stocks are actually real companies, or simply created for the purpose of a short-lived but explosive ride on the stock market is debatable. But who cares, right? If you can begin to predict the roller coaster stock patterns of these 'fictitious' companies you can cash in on incredible earnings.

Let's take a look at the typical result once a penny stock announcement arrives in your email in-box.

1. The announcement "Our new pick. ABCD could double in the next 24 hours!"

2. Now start watching the stock. Save its chart as a bookmark and watch it over the period of a week two. What typically happens is the first announcement is made early in the morning, and when the trading

day opens the stock is up 50% or more from the prior day. Clearly the announcers manipulated this rise and announced it before you had the chance to get in on the first peak. No matter, as a rule there will be a second or third peak after a 20% or more drop, and often some more 20%+ peaks and valleys after that as you get updated 'tips' on the stock 'about to explode' in your email inbox.

3. Watch for (or set a buy order) for a drop of about 20% from the original peak, and watch for (or set a sell order) for a rise above your buy point of 10%. This is a conservative strategy to get a 10% increase in a matter of days. If you want to be more aggressive, set a buy order at 30% or more drop from the original peak, and a sell order at a 20% rise above the 30% valley. Typically there will be a series of peaks and valleys in the two weeks following announcement, after which the stock often begins a slow drift towards zero.

In a nutshell:

When you get the initial email announcement of some mystery stock about to skyrocket, go to the chart, put in a <u>limit buy order</u> about 20% below the current peak, and a <u>limit sell order</u> 10-15% above your buy point.

Let's look at an actual penny stock chart below in the two weeks following its announcement on the web.

At about 5am on day one (Friday on the chart) I received an email announcing that this stock had just gone up 500%, so I checked its chart first thing in the morning. It had gone up 500% in the afternoon prior to the announcement. Obviously the 'insiders' had manipulated the surge prior to announcing it, so they could announce 'a 500% surge' to get people's attention at a public announcement and people would start buying it.

Note that at the Friday post, the stock was at 0.18. On Thursday prior to the public email it was closer to 0.04. Of course no one had the opportunity to get in on the 500% surge, because the announcement was made after this first surge had already happened. So at the start of Friday it is at 0.18.

It goes up to 0.19 in the first hour, then down to 17.5 and then up to 19.5 by the end of the trading day. That was the first valley/peak, but from my observations of various penny stocks, the second valley/peak will often be greater and more reliable than the first, or third/fourth peak. Again this is just an observation.

At the opening of the Friday trade day in this case, my strategy would suggest putting in a buy order at about 0.15 and a sell order at about 0.17; An expectation that the stock is going to tank 30% or more following the initial peak, and then rebound up 15-20% within a day or two.

Note that is exactly what happens. With a limit buy order at .15 (about 20% below the initial peak of .18), and a limit sell order at .17 (about 15% above the valley at .15) you make 15% on this stock in one day. Now you sit on your winnings until the next penny stock announcement. Typically, as in this stock, there are maybe two rebounds of 20+% in the week or two after the initial announcement and peak, after which point the stock begins a predictable downslope from which it never recovers. From my observations, after the second peak the valleys and peaks are not as predictable, e.g. on my second bid using this penny stock system I tried to cash in on a fourth peak that never happened, so I learned my lesson. Not to say that the third and fourth peaks won't happen; sometimes they do, e.g. in this case skyrocketing to over 600% from the first day you could have bought it following the initial announcement.

However, notice in this stock that there is a second valley on Tuesday of the next week at about 0.18, after which it climbs back up to 0.26. **In the next week the stock skyrockets to over $1.30, over a 600% rise from after it was announced at $0.19 on the Friday prior.** From my observations however this is atypical, i.e. a series of 20-30% valleys followed by a 15-20% surge is more normal, after which the stock trails off to oblivion. Obviously these penny stocks make surges and valleys far more explosive than the Dow or most major stocks. Can you be happy making 10%-20% in a week? Watch the penny stock market and cash in on what seems to be a definite roller coaster ride and almost routine and predictable surge/crash pattern.

The simple trick seems to be:

Get in early after the initial announcement and don't get too greedy. Be happy with a 10 or 15% gain in the first week after announcement. Bidding on 3rd or 4th peaks can be extremely successful if you predict correctly, but may also be more risky. Safer is probably, after your first 10-15% gain, to just wait for the next mystery stock pick tip to arrive in your email inbox and go after the early surges.

---

[1] Reproduced with permission of Yahoo! Inc. ©2011 Yahoo! Inc. YAHOO! and the YAHOO! logo are registered trademarks of Yahoo! Inc.

Good luck with this suggested strategy, now enjoy my novel on penny stock manipulation below.

A NOVEL: INSIDE THE INSIDERS
By Jerry Greene
All applicable copyright rights reserved 2008.

THEME: 'Wall Street' meets '21' meets 'The Net'.

PLOT OUTLINE: Three bright college kids (two boys, one girl), at an elite college that grooms many high end lawyers and Wall Street types, become enticed by the possibility inserting themselves into the world of stock manipulation and insider trading. They are drawn into a world that is over their head and begin to mess with a ruthless organized crime faction group of serious stock manipulators who are in it for millions. An escalating game of cat and mouse, computer intrigue, and increasing risk and potential for high profits ensues, with Winslow, Gretchen, and Bergen wondering if they ever should have ever made their first penny stock bid.

CHAPTER ONE

Winslow pedaled up the winding path on the hill leading up to campus. It was one of the first cool days of fall and his bicycle tires crunched through the handful of paper dry leaves that had already dropped from the trees. One thing Winslow liked about the fall was that you could start wearing jeans again. He had been wearing shorts pretty much every day for the last six months, and as much as he liked shorts, it felt good to have jeans on. The perfect pair of jeans almost felt dressy, and he had searched around for a couple of perfect jeans and he was wearing one of the pairs today. He also had slip on vans on, after a summer of wearing crocs.

Neither vans nor crocs were popular on campus, but Winslow was bucking the trend and found them both comfortable and practical. The popular shoes were flip flops and suede snow boots, and on most spring and fall days you could see groups of students with flip flops side by side with snow boots. Winslow recognized the irony that fashion often trumped common sense, as if the temperature was good for flip flops it was too warm for snow boots, and visa versa, but no shoe in the middle temperature range had seemed to catch on at most colleges. Even at this elite college, fashion and following the popular trends however irrational dominated student behavior about as strongly as it had in high school.

It took either brains or money to get into this college, and many of the students had both. Winslow hadn't done that well grade wise in high school, B average; he didn't really see the point of trying too hard in high school, and his family wasn't wealthy, but somehow his head was exceptionally clear on the day of his SAT's and he had nailed them. 1450+ could just about solely get you into this school, and when his SAT scores arrived, his parents had pushed him to apply to this school, especially since he was in state and could get in state tuition rates.

He was now mingling with students from all over the country who had picked this school as a top choice, and the attitudes of many of them coming from generations of money and influence was way different from what Winslow had grown up with at his local high school. He was managing so far to mix in ok, especially since his high school girlfriend had also made it in, making them two of the four from their school who had made it in to this nationally ranked liberal arts school, rather than just the state university in the neighboring metropolis.

Financially, Winslow had a partial academic and need scholarship, and a partial tennis scholarship, and while he wasn't eating free at the athletic cafeteria, and no one was offering him a car or condo, he planned to make it out with not much more than a years salary worth of school loan debt. His girlfriend Gretchen could have gotten a full tennis scholarship at many schools in the country, including this one if she pushed for it, but her family didn't really need it, so they had settled for the ½ tuition scholarship the college had offered. Gretchen's family was significantly wealthier than Winslow's and she was usually at number two on the tennis team, compared to Winslow's #3 or 4 position. Also the college had a fully funded woman's tennis team, compared to only a partially funded men's team, as a Title 9 compromise to adjust for the highly funded men's football team. All together Winslow had to be significantly more careful how he spent his money than Gretchen, but when they did things together they usually did things that fit within Winslow's budget since he didn't want to be carried on the back of his more wealthier friends.

Winslow's bike edged up the last incline to the plateau the college was built on. As he pedaled onto 'the flats' as many students called them he turned onto the diagonal concrete path crossing the grass library quad. Students were going this way and that on the parallel and diagonal paths. It was a pedestrian and bicycle friendly paradise of paths, like most college campuses, and Winslow cherished his commute. "I hope I can always commute like this", he thought, realizing that a few years out of college the commute for most graduates wouldn't be quite so idyllic.

At this time of the morning many of the students were headed towards one of the on-campus mini coffee bars that had been franchised at about ten locations on campus. The caffeine industry recognized that college was a good time to initiate a lifetime of coffee-every-morning habit, and the coffee bars had caught on as strongly as flip flops and snow boots. Winslow hadn't bucked that trend, and like most students his satchel had two bottle pockets, one for a coffee mug, and one for a water bottle. If there was one time in life that you needed a really functional pack or shoulder satchel it was college, and Winslow had spent a long time looking for the perfect one; brown canvas with a wide shoulder strap, large volume main compartment, two bottle sleeves, and a bunch of smaller zippered pockets. As Winslow sort of glanced at his satchel, jeans, and vans he thought to himself that this was a generation, especially during college, where men could put as much thought into accessorizing as women.

The thick trunk oak and maple trees that dotted the quad and the rest of the campus were the deciduous equivalent of old growth. A few choice ones had been spared and nurtured when the campus had been erected and had grown over the years into knarred and solitary giants, each commanding an intersection of the various sidewalks and paths. During most of the summer students wore spots in the grass for studying and socializing, but now in the fall morning their shadows were long and wide across the grass, and the few students who were sitting on the grass were seeking out the sunny areas. Later in the day there would be girls in swimsuits laying out for the last bit of tan before winter set in, along with guys without shirts throwing footballs and Frisbees, with the occasional girl mixed in.

Winslow never studied outside, he felt it too hard to concentrate, and he never just laid out in the sun either. He got enough sun playing tennis. It seemed like for some students tanning was a minor academic degree. They laid out in the sun until the snow started falling, and then on December and Spring Breaks returned from some tropic destination sporting a deep summer tan on their faces and arms, and still wearing their flip flops to show off the tan on their feet. Winslow figured these would be the ones who still at 60 or 70, as brown and wrinkled as a paper grocery bag, would still be going for a darker tan in retirement on a beach somewhere.

Winslow glanced at his watch noting that he would be exactly on time to meet Gretchen and fill up their coffee mugs before going to their first class; one of the several on their schedule that they both had signed up for; Stock and Security Law. Both of them were undergraduates, but the college had a liberal policy of allowing even freshmen to take some upper division classes that focused on a specific pursuit, deliberately to allow them to see into a career before they formally decided on a career path or declared a major. In this class, although Gretchen and Winslow were both only juniors, most of the students in the class were law students and MBA's. Ironically enough, Winslow noted, some of his undergraduate courses were often more difficult than the graduate courses he elected to take each semester.

Winslow glanced at his watch again as he pulled up to the building where the café was, noticing that he was just one minute late from when he said he would meet Gretchen. He made a habit of being punctual, in fact college forced one to be more punctual than life after college; you had to be pretty much exactly on time at least five times per day for classes, a more rigid schedule than most people had to deal with regularly in the work world. One thing Winslow liked about the forced punctuality was the dependence on a watch, another accessory he was proud of. Downtown at lunch hour you could see many corporate neckties wearing a watch similar to what Winslow had. In fact he had spent a couple of noon hours downtown watching the executives in suits and deciding on which watch to wear. "Might as well dress the part", he thought, realizing that image and people skills were often far important than academic learning once you hit the job market. This watch had cost a couple hundred dollars, but he planned on it lasting many years, and it gave him a professional appearance, even in jeans.

He parked his bike next to a full bike rack and simply locked the wheel to the frame with a U-lock. While his bike was entirely functional, it was under $500 and he had more or less made it look deliberately beat up, in other words no one was going to steal it, not while there were plenty of high profile bikes on the rack near by. Winslow never saw the sense in getting a $2000 mountain bike to ride around campus, although many students could afford it and they were used to a life of always having the best, so there were plenty of bikes in that category on the rack next to his. And while a percentage of those bikes disappeared each semester from campus or porches and driveways, Winslow's bike had never been bothered.

Gretchen was at the counter when he walked in. "I forgot. Who is buying today", Winslow asked.

"Since I can't remember it is probably me", Gretchen replied, "Hand me your mug you slacker."

"I am always a slacker before I get my coffee." Winslow said.

"Two coffees", Gretchen told the counter employee, "We brought our own mugs, and plenty of room for cream, please".

Many students opted for the specialty coffee drinks; latte, espresso, au lait, cappuccino, but Winslow had talked Gretchen into going just for straight house coffee. "It's all caffeine", Winslow had said, "So why pay twice as much for it blended a different way or so you can watch the mixer go through all the amazing and exciting steps in making it." Gretchen had finally agreed to the simpler option, which easily saved them each $40/

month, and Winslow sometimes carried hot chocolate packets that they poured their mugs for their own economy mochas.

Winslow handed Gretchen his coffee mug and pulled a packet of hot chocolate out of his satchel.

"Thanks for the coffee, I've got the mocha component covered", he grinned.

"Always cheap", Gretchen commented wryly.

"Practical by necessity", Winslow corrected. "Someday I won't need to be carrying my own chocolate packets."

"You probably still will be even when you're on Wall Street" Gretchen said.

"Uh yeah, you are probably right", Winston replied, "Maybe it will become a trend, but then all trends start out as someone's nutball idea before they catch on."

"Trendsetter or nutball, that is the common dilemma that most of us have when trying to describe you" Gretchen answered smiling.

"I of course have exactly no problem being an enigma to the bulk of humanity", Winslow said as they exited the building.

"I won't dispute that indisputable fact", Gretchen answered.

CHAPTER TWO

Gretchen and Winslow meandered their way through the thickening path of students trying to make it to 9am classes. Bikes, skateboards, and pedestrians maneuvered for position creating various streams and side currents of motion, choreographed in real time as everyone pushed on towards some darkened classroom where their minds would receive a dizzying influx of information, how much relevant to later life, debatable. Brains working overtime just for the sake of learning, or something of more tangible value?

"Just think", Winslow said, "In a couple of years all these same people will be doing this same dance, only in cars."

They walked up the stairs and into the building and through the few hallways that led to the classroom. This was one of the smaller classrooms with stadium style seating, each row of chairs a little higher than the one in front so you could see over the students who were sitting in front of you. Most of the undergraduate classrooms were stadium style holding up to 200 students, and many of the graduate classrooms were small and non-tiered like high school classrooms. There were a number sort of in the middle tiered stadium style that could hold a maximum of 50 students. There were about 35 students in this Stock and Security law class. Although students could sit where ever they liked, as in most classes most students had informally gravitated to a seat during the first couple of lectures and the seats had more or less become as fixed as assigned seating. Winslow and Gretchen had in the first class picked near the window in a row near the back of the class, and had kept coming to those seats since.

While many professors at this school often used the Socratic method, continually questioning students and creating a dialogue, this professor wasn't one of them. He had a well-organized multi-media presentation, usually using power-point and a laser pointer and only infrequently looking up from his notes and power point screen to peer around the class, almost as if to assure himself that there were actually still students in the classroom. His name was Miles Sanford.

While the material had enough depth and detail and facts in terms of laws and cases and actual security fraud events that had happened, Sanford was kind enough to basically let everyone know what was likely to be on the exams. After lecturing and gesturing at the screen he would stop about every ten minutes or so and say, "Now this is going to be important." For students who didn't isolate themselves from the academic social scene, and who bothered to try to get the inside scoop on how professors tested, it was widely know that that phrase "going to be important" might as well be "going to be on the exam." In short if you highlighted in your notes every place Sanford said that, and focused on studying those items before the test, you could usually sail through the exams fairly easily. There were other classes where there was way less actual information, but it was a guess as to what was actually going to be on the exams. Winslow found it a monstrous waste to be spending months and $10,000's of dollars on classes that in terms of actual useful information could be summarized in a ten page paper and common sense. This class wasn't one of them, and the professor had streamlined his approach to impart the maximum exchange of usable information in the 14-week format.

Today's lecture was focusing on a couple of real-life scenarios of stock manipulation, what had been done that was legal and illegal, and who had gained and lost from the scheme. The key point was that if you had enough money to through at some very low end stock, and the money didn't have to be your own, you could get the stock to rise artificially, and this was being done in the real world with the insiders often making a killing on the backs of innocent investors who mostly lost. Winslow watched the graphs and the laser pointer as the professor spoke about the rise and fall of a penny stock that had recently been manipulated. While the professor described the kinds of losses the innocent investors had incurred, and seemed to have some sympathy for that, when he described the gains made by the manipulators it seemed that he was subtly infatuated by the brilliance of it. Sanford seemed to be trying to hide this, and Winslow had suggested his infatuation to a couple of other students who shrugged it off, Winslow was convinced that the brilliance of hovering on the fence of what was legal and what was illegal and making a huge profit off of it was something Sanford never failed to notice. It was a topic he and Gretchen often talked about after class, and while she had called him nuts to start out with she now agreed with him totally.

"I didn't agree with you at first," she had said, "but after his little side-bar lecture on the banking computer tech that had made a couple hundred thousand by transferring fraction of a cent transactions into a separate account it was obvious. He didn't seem too outraged by it" There was some rumor that Sanford had been in a $400,000 year position in a wall street firm, and had gotten caught in some scheme that was borderline stock fraud, tech fraud, but to keep it quiet, and since whether or not any laws had been broken was questionable, the firm had allowed him to quietly 'retire' with grace, and with an inside connection to a teaching job at this university via a crony of one of the firms associates.

The pace of this Sanford's lectures was slow and organized enough that students didn't need to be so rapidly scribbling notes that there was no time to actually watch the lecture. The smart professors realized that part being successful at teaching was providing enjoyable entertainment, if the students enjoyed the show you got good reviews, and there was no better way than to mess up the entertainment factor than lecturing so fast that students couldn't just sit back and watch on occasion. The proper way to succeed in Simpson's class, and enjoy the process, was to just watch while he was leading up to the main points, and then carefully take notes whenever he said, "Now this will be important." Simpson intentionally paused after making his major points, thus allowing students ample time to write it down. He also referred often to sections of the textbook and recommended that students highlight them. "What you need to bring to this class", he had said, "outside of paper and pencil, is your textbook and a highlighter." This method along with his, "Now this will be important", and technique substantially reduced the amount of note taking over other classes.

Winslow had noticed and appreciated the reduced note taking factor of this class, and realized that one of the most important study skills was seeing inside the professor's brain, how they think in terms of lecture design, and how this would be translated into exam design. Winslow had successfully done this for most of his classes, and always was able to keep ahead and do well on exams.

One of his favorite techniques during study groups before exams was to tell the other students what questions he guessed would be on the exam. He was often happy to open his exams to see several of the exact questions he had predicted. Gretchen and a few of their other routine study group students had began to notice how often Winslow was right, and had begun to really take heed of Winslow's exam question predictions. When Winslow said, "Here is a question that I think will be on the exam", in many classes, it was almost as obviously important in predictive value as when Sanford said, "Now this will be important."

There were a couple of students who regularly went up to talk to Sanford at his podium after class, as there were in most classes, but Winslow was never one of these. Today a different student was up at the podium outside of the regular 'teacher's pets' and Sanford appeared to by wryly grinning at that students comments as he shuffled papers and fielded questions from the regular podium group. The brief exchange ended and the student walked away leaving the podium regulars still chatting with Sanford. This new student also sat next to the window, a couple of rows in front of Winslow and Gretchen, and generally appeared to take less notes and appear more distracted than the average student. He had never asked a question in class, never seemed to leave class with any other students, and seemed to spend a lot of time gazing out the window and then just returning to his notebook to write down the important points that Sanford always led up to.

As Winslow and Gretchen filed out of the room through the throng of students they found themselves behind the new student who had been at the podium. Winslow didn't often approach other students after this class, as him and Gretchen usually just talked to each other unless one of the other study group students came up, but Winslow had found something about this new guy to be intriguing so he sort of pressed forward to be close enough to make a comment and then said, "So how is this class going for you?"

"Oh, you know, piece of cake", the other student replied. "I try to avoid the difficult and useless classes if I can help it, although they do make you take some of them."

"Agreed", Winslow replied, "Academically challenge as many useless classes as you can, and petition to avoid as many as you can't challenge, is my philosophy"

"Not just blindly following the rest of the cattle I see", the other student countered, "I'm Ethan Bergen by the way".

"I am Gretchen and this is Winslow", Gretchen introduced herself into the conversation. "Pleased to meet you."

"Likewise", said Ethan, "by the way my small handful of friends, most who aren't at this college, call me Bergen."

"Ok" said Winslow, "Bergen, Gretchen, and Winslow. I guess we all agree, the names have been changed to protect the innocent."

CHAPTER THREE

At the after class introduction the three had agreed to meet at 4pm after their 3pm classes. Winslow had suggested one of the caffeine stops on campus, but Gretchen had argued for a walk.

"I don't want to go sit somewhere after sitting all day", she said, "I need some exercise. Recess was a good idea when we were in grade school, and it is still a good idea. Imagine the whole campus coming outside to play for a half an hour before lunch, or for that matter the same for the working third of America. The Chinese do it. Imagine the whole country outside throwing footballs and frisbees from 12 to 12:30."

No one could dispute the perfect image of her logic so they settled on a bike ride up to the hills that overlooked campus and then sitting and watching rush hour from the eagle and mountain lion point of view.

"So what do you think of Sanford's stock law class?" said Winslow, "How much do you study for it?"

"I like it" said Bergen, "Very organized. No tricks or surprises on the exams. And as for studying I make it a habit to never study more than two hours per night, total for all my classes, and usually just for one hour. I don't want to kill myself doing this."

"Alright" said Gretchen, "Another potential member of our potential anti-study group. Some people are part of study groups, but we are trying to put together an anti-study group. A handful of students to streamline the key info needed for exams and share it with the group so we all walk in there equally prepared on the same info. As long as everyone has good insight on what the important points are we should be able to cut this down to the minimum work required for everyone."

"That is her dream" said Winslow, "I am of the belief that college will be hard no matter how you try to trim the study time fat. We are not met to have fun or relaxation now. We are meant to have a headache full of information at all times."

"Sorry pal" said Bergen, "It looks like the anti-study group has a consensus. Study as little as possible to do as well enough in each class. Fly with the eagles or eat off the floor with the turkeys. I am down."

"Sweet" said Gretchen, "I knew we would eventually meet a couple more irreverent student types."

"What are we doing" said Winslow, "Creating a pact right before our very eyes that spits in the face of traditional academic morals? I suppose you guys are going to shake hands or something."

Gretchen grabbed Winslow's hand and pulled it in to the center. "You too loser" she said.

Bergen plopped his hand on top of theirs and squeezed, "Study less, have more fun" he said.

As they sat their on a rock overlooking the city, their hands clasped in a group handshake, they watched the daylight fading and lights from houses and cars become more intense. The roads and freeway sparkled with hundreds of steadily moving pairs of lights; humans inside their motorized and wheeled glass and metal terrariums inching along the concrete paths leading them home or to somewhere to shop for the perfect home accessories. Gretchen, Winslow, and Bergen were glad to be where they were; watching industrialized, material pursuit society from the caveman's vantage point.

CHAPTER FOUR

Now that Winslow and Gretchen had broken the ice with Bergen, Bergen would always bound up to them after Sanford's class to remark on whatever devious market manipulation, tech fraud, or insider investment tip violation case that Sanford had discussed during the lecture, and the various high tech tracking systems the feds had used to discover and trap the violators.

In today's lecture Sanford had discussed also how sophisticated the insider traders and manipulators had become in the use of software, hardware, and legal tricks to try to stay one step of the feds. "It is usually just a matter of time" Sandford said, "before the stock schemers get too greedy or too careless and the feds catch up with them." Nonetheless it seemed like a game of cat and mouse where, because of the enormous amount of money that could be made by capitalizing on the greed of 'honest' investors, the mice often had a lot of money to throw at technology, middle men and lawyers, to stay ahead of the insider trading and fraud task forces. When Sanford discussed the various methods the mice used it was almost like there was a gleam in his eye. Probably most of the students hadn't noticed it, but Gretchen, Winslow, and Bergen had developed a keen eye for it, and none of them had any doubts anymore.

When Winslow had offered his hypothesis to Bergen on Sanford's infatuation with the intricacies of beating the system and staying one step ahead of the law, he was surprised that it took no effort to make his point as it had with Gretchen; Bergen had been noticing it all along, and even had noticed more events and statements in Sanford's class than Winslow has. This was one of those days when Bergen had noticed even another example, and he was as usual, brimming with energy to discuss the full ramifications with his two new pals.

"This is such a sweet and dangerous game all these guys are playing" Bergen said, "I want to graduate tomorrow so I can be part of it. The whole thing is like poker, like Texas Hold 'Em, a few cards are up for everyone to see, everyone has a few cards they can only see themselves, and everyone is trying to guess what you are holding and what is going to be secret is going to be turned up on the next card. The feds are the cat, the inside traders and manipulators are the mouse."

As they walked out of the building into the sunny fall day Bergen let his words sink in. He wouldn't be proposing this type of conversation to anyone he didn't trust, or to anyone who didn't have the type of irreverence that often went with the upper percentiles of traditional and scientifically measured intelligence. Gretchen and Winslow weren't as much on the fringe as he was, but he knew they leaned in the same direction, and he was glad to have the potential to draw some other minds into the darker reaches of his imagination. Besides it was Friday, Time to let your brain relax and step out of the mold a little for a couple of days.

"What if a third party entered in?" He speculated, "Between the cat and the mouse, but with an entirely different motive? Not money, not to further your career in law enforcement, but just for the fun of it, you know, just to wreak a little havoc?"

"I hope you're not suggesting a third party that some of us know", Winslow countered, "I think we have more important things to do, like graduating."

"I am not suggesting we do anything", said Bergen, "I am just suggesting we go get a coffee and have a hypothetical conversation. You really don't think that I would actually suggest that we deviate from our studies to do something insidious do you?"

"The king of rhetorical questions as always" said Gretchen, "You guys can hatch your plots without me if you want. I have tennis practice. There is a match this weekend and I have a little glitch in my forehand I need to correct. I'll catch up with you guys after the match tomorrow. Any one want to buy me a drink Saturday night?"

"It would be our pleasure" said Bergen speaking for the both of them.

"Sure" said Winslow, "I wouldn't mind hitting with you for an hour tonight if you think it would help your forehand."

"Definitely", said Gretchen, "Some laid back recreational tennis always helps me loosen up for matches. See you guys later."

Winslow and Bergen watched her trot off across the quad.

"Tennis gives you good legs." Bergen remarked.

"I know", said Winslow, "Why do you think I play?"

"To meet girls with good legs?" said Bergen.

Winslow considered the misinterpretation of his intent but decided not to object. "Hey it's worked so far, all the way from junior high school to now".

Winslow and Bergen hopped on their bikes and rode into town to grab a beer. Winslow's favorite place to unwind was a dark Mexican restaurant; in fact he liked Mexican restaurants in general because chips and salsa were the expected rule for before you even ordered. What other type of restaurant had that kind of policy? Another thing Winslow liked about Mexican was beans. Beans were just about the healthiest single thing you could get eating out, or even at home or fast food. Fiber was the only nutritional component generally deficient in the American diet, and beans had about twice the amount of fiber as anything else; e.g. the fiber content of fruits, vegetables, grains, and oatmeal was well below that found in beans. Winslow often recalled the story in Hemmingway's "Tortilla Flat" where the school nurse finds out that the poor Mexican kids eat beans and tortillas for breakfast, lunch and dinner, but she nonetheless finds them as healthy as any of the kids in school. Winslow and Bergen had sat down in a booth, and within minutes they each had a glass of water, a beer, and a bowl of chips and salsa.

"I have intentionally got myself on a number of the spam stock email lists", started Bergen, "And what I have noticed is that the spam stocks take a dive about a day or two after the stock tip hits the email list, and then within the next day they rebound as much as 50% before beginning their descent into fractions of cents values. As well as the initial mass buy wave that the manipulators and their investors are riding, there is a secondary wave not as big as the first one, but rideable anyway. I think we should try it."

"That sounds amazingly great and interesting", answered Winslow, "But doesn't it assume we have something we don't have, i.e. money?"

"You have money for the semester from your student loan right?" said Bergen, "I have like $5000 still for the rest of the semester. I've been watching the pattern for a while, and I don't think we are going to lose, so I think we should each commit half of our semester funds, so a total of $5000. If we lose we live cheap and get a couple of credit cards to live off of until we graduate and can pay them back. It's not like there aren't plenty of credit card companies marketing on campus that would love to sign us up for a lifetime of living beyond our means. Come on pal. Be an American."

"How about $1000?" Winslow tried to negotiate for less risk.

"Not worth it", replied Bergen, "Come on $2500 each. It's not like we are going to lose all of it. We won't be too greedy. We will set it up so that we get out at a 20% profit, or $1000 in winnings, and we put in a sell order if it drops 20% so we hopefully can't lose more than $1000."

"Oh, right a sure thing in the stock market. Those happen all the time. And you never get burned. I watched 'Wall Street'. You are starting to sound like a cold call stock broker." Winslow expressed his doubts.

Bergen set down his beer, wiped the chip salt off his hands and reached into his bag to pull out his laptop. He flipped it open and opened up an icon on his desktop. "Ok, check this out", he said as he rotated the computer towards Winslow.

Winslow looked at the series of graphs on the screen, saved one per page. The trend was obvious. Each of the penny stocks had shown an exponential growth phase in the days leading up to the spam email announcement to entice innocent investors, had abruptly tanked by about 60% a few days afterward, but each showed a 20-30% rebound about a day later before tanking again and beginning a gradual descent to near zero.

"I am on all the lists", Bergen said, "I get about two of these email alerts a day. We could invest in something tonight if you are up for it." He rotated the laptop back to face himself and pressed a few buttons.

"Look at this one', he said, "PHYS.pk. I just got the announcement this afternoon, trading at $1.20 last month, jumped to $2.80 in the last couple of days. I say we put in a buy at about $1.20, it should drop to there in two days, and then we set a stop sell at say $1.60. Most everyone else out there will be far more greedy, and their loss is our gain. I already have the on-line trading account set up. I just need to put some more funds in it, $2500 each. Come on pal. Take a step out of boredom. You must admit, we have got the brains to do this right if anyone does." Bergen grabbed his beer and took a sip and began munching on the chips again. He held a chip in his hand with a large chunk of salsa perched on it, and stared intently but warmly at Winslow. "What do you say?" he completed his thought as he shoved the chip into his mouth and followed it with a swallow of beer.

"Come on finish your beer and let's go to your apartment", Bergen completed his pitch.

Winslow sat back feeling the slight relaxation of the first beer and the comfort of the restaurant booth. "What the heck", he said. "I guess the cost benefit ratio is decent if you figure in the excitement factor. You are taking the lead on this though just so there is no misinterpretation as to how this all got started further down the road. Got it?"

Bergen nodded, "No problem, just happy to have anyone to share my schemes with."

They left some money on the table, each took a last sip of water, signaled at the waitress, and then walked out of the restaurant.

CHAPTER FIVE

Winslow and Bergen had now over the last couple of weeks followed their 'second wave' plan bidding on spam email stock tips that Bergen had been receiving, they had lost about 20% on two of the penny stocks, but had made up to 20-30% on six others and their initial $5000 was now at about $11,000. Winslow had been arguing to stock pile each of their $2500 back into their school credit union bank account, but Bergen had so far been able to talk him out of it.

Both of them were having a hard time concentrating in classes in general, and this current business math class that they were taking together had been no exception. As they excited the building into the late afternoon fall sun Bergen bounded up to Winslow in his usual excited manner, "While most of the campus is getting tattoos and wearing flip flops, we are up the skirt of the stock market. Doesn't that excite you?"

Winslow remarked wryly, "The skirt part does."

"Let's go back to your apartment and bid on another one", said Bergen, "Hot tip today. GLRS.pk. Up 64% from last week. Can't miss."

"Sure", replied Winslow, "With two conditions. One I get to transfer $3500 back into my regular bank account, and this is permanently untouchable after this. With the extra $1000 I can cruise through the rest of the semester and take Gretchen to the Gulf over break. You are invited also of course." By the Gulf Winslow meant the Gulf of Mexico, either on the Texas side or the north east corner of Mexico. The water was warm, and prices were cheap most months except spring break.

"I can live with that Bergen replied, "Especially with the invitation. I'll transfer $3500 back to my account also. What is the second condition?"

"I was going to say that you let me have more time to study", replied Winslow, "But on second thought, I won't make that a condition. I am making it through Ok and I'll just take the time when I need it. But here is an alternate second condition. We don't get Gretchen involved, OK?"

"Well I promise to not try and drag her in, but you know me, I want to talk about it just for the pure conversation value", Bergen explained. "Besides, I have already told her a little. And you know her. She will want to know more."

Winslow felt good that he had been able to at least negotiate for the safety valve of taking their initial funds out, plus enough for a vacation, so he let his face relax a little. Gretchen knew a little obviously. They would share more when he offered her the Gulf trip. It would be fun to be all three lounging on a beach somewhere, on a free ride from their innocent dabbling in the low ideals end of the stock market, knowing that they had played, won, and would get out soon and be able to fondly look back at the whole experience.

"Sure", he finally said, "Glad to see that you are a reasonable guy, at least at your best moments. It gives me faith."

Winslow and Bergen climbed the stairs to Winslow's apartment. He unlocked the door to his apartment, sat his satchel down, and went to grab a water bottle by the sink. He had sink faucet water purifier, and had a habit of keeping two or three water bottles of purified water around the apartment so he could easily grab a sip whenever he felt the least bit thirsty. He knew from playing tennis that it was never good to get dehydrated and drinking even a little at the first sign of thirst had a general health payback that was well worth it.

He offered Bergen a bottle and then walked over to his desk. It had an identical laptop PC to the one he carried in his satchel. He had bought them both at the same time when there was a substantial mail in rebate offer, and he had them both set up virtually identically. If one crashed for some reason, he could simply use the other one temporarily, and after wiping the crashed one clean, the alternate one could be used to restore any programs and files that had been deleted. Winslow had hooked up the second computer and the boys hunkered down at the desk with the light from the computers illuminating their faces. Bergen had pulled up the GLRS.pk profile on one of the computers and Winslow had opened up a window on the other to their online stock trade account.

"First things first", said Winslow as he moved the mouse and entered values to transfer $3500 out of the stock trade account back into his college bank account. When he finished he turned to Bergen. "You too pal."

Bergen smiled wryly and replied, "I knew you weren't going to let me forget about that part of the promise. Alright let me get a second window open and transfer my $3500 also." Bergen deftly worked the mouse, using his memorized password to open his stock trade account and mirrored Winslow's steps. Winslow watched as if he needed to confirm to believe that Bergen would actually do it and was finally satisfied to see Bergen's trading account drop $3500, the same as his. "Satisfied?" Bergen said at the end of the procedure.

Bergen clicked back to the GLRS page and noticed that it was currently at $2.20 per share, up from $1.40 two days before. "Let's buy at $1.60 and sell at either $1.10 stop loss or $1.90 whichever comes first OK?" he said to Winslow without looking.

"Your driving as always", Winslow replied, "I got my investment back plus. I am an innocent bystander at this point."

Bergen nodded and begin plugging in the buy and sell values. When he had the screen verified at all the chosen parameters he motioned Winslow to take a look. "Look good to you he said?" Winslow nodded also and Bergen clicked the send button.

After they saw all the values go through, and they had each checked their active account folders, Bergen leaned back in his chair. It had been exciting up to now, and he was reluctant to let the excitement drop off. He had been wondering about the people out their setting up and manipulating the stocks, and for the majority of investors who were loosing out by trying to catch the first wave which rarely if ever materialized. Finally he commented, "Let's monkey with the monikers."

"What do you mean exactly?" asked Winslow.

"We have got a blanket list these stock tips have been sent to." Bergen formulated, "Let's send out our own tips on these stocks, lets say, 'ignore the 1st wave and catch the 2nd'. That should get the attention of someone."

"And we want to get the attention of someone why?" Winslow asked, "I thought this was all low profile. If we advise the innocent investors to try to beat the spammers at their own game I don't think the spammers will like us anymore."

"Look", replied Bergen, "We have our money back and then some. I don't think you and I are just going to this college to make money are we? I mean, we are hoping to make a lot of money obviously, but we also have grander more ethical goals. To do something interesting, to be proud of our achievements, and to not hurt anyone along the way, right? The spammers out there we are dealing with have no such clean aspect to their motives.

They are just trying to make tons of money and not get caught, but the fact that they are stepping on and crushing the dreams of others just does not figure into their equation. Let's go after them just to prove to ourselves that we are above them. We know the Feds are after them right? If things get too hot we'll just spill our beans to the Feds. We are the good guys, the Feds are the law, and the spammers are, well, the criminal faction, they're basically organized crime, in fact that is exactly what they are, an organized crime faction. In fact that is what I am calling them from now on, the organized crime faction, the OCF."

Bergen looked intently at Winslow, and after he realized from Winslow's quiet gaze that a reply wasn't immediately coming he got up from his chair and wandered into the kitchen to see if there were two beers in the fridge. The apartment was dark except for the blue light from the two computer screens, and the yellow stove light in the kitchen. When he opened the door of the fridge he was bathed in white light in the dark backdrop of the apartment. "Perfect", he mumbled to himself as he saw two remaining bottles of beer on the shelf. He grabbed them, shut the refrigerator door, walked back into the living room and handed one of the beers to Winslow, and remained standing as he opened his beer and took the first swallow.

Winslow paused for a moment before opening his beer, watching Bergen rock back and forth and look down at him. "You know what I think? Said Winslow as he twisted off the cap of his beer, "You don't really care about the money. You just get off on messing with people."

Bergen chuckled, and rocked back and forth on each leg a little more vigorously.

Winslow continued, "Have you ever tried to look inside your psyche and ask 'Where does that twisted little personality defect come from'?"

Bergen kept his focus, but digested Winslow's comment, "You know what I love about you?

"What?" Winslow said.

"That you notice that about me!" Bergen sat happily back down in the chair next to Winslow and slapped him on the shoulder.

Winslow looked at him squarely, "You mean you've been with other people who didn't notice?

Bergen paused for a moment meeting Winslow's gaze and then turned back to the computer screen, "Most of the world only notices something when it is on fire, in their lap, and biting a chunk out of their leg. Let's get to work. I can't wait to piss the OCF monkeys off. We give everyone a tip on how to catch the second wave, and the result will be that fewer and fewer will bid on the non-existent first wave, thus the whole OCF scheme will dry up. Doesn't it make you feel like we are doing are part for the greater good of humanity?" Bergen tilted his head with the question and waited for what he knew would be Winslow's response.

"As usual you have my king trapped", Winslow said, "When I find a way to win any of these arguments I will let you know."

CHAPTER SIX

It had been about a week since Winslow and Bergen had started sending emails to alert the investors on the mass list, and Winslow had recently noticed his home laptop running a little slower than usual. He also had a vague feeling that someone had been in his apartment, although he couldn't really put his finger on it. It had seemed like some of the papers and books on his desk had been slightly out of place but he couldn't be sure. He had told Bergen about it and Bergen thought he should come over to take a look. As they rode bikes towards Winslow's apartment at the noon break between classes they pondered how to examine Winslow's apartment and laptop to see if they had somehow been directly tracked by the OCF.

They rode through 'the flats' and began descending down the hill into one of the neighborhoods populated mostly by either graduate or 3rd and 4th year students. The younger classes often preferred the more popular party atmosphere of 'the hill' on the other side of campus. The ride was pleasant, and as nervous as Winslow was of the possibility that some ruthless faction had crept into their quiet college life, he always enjoyed these rides and conversations with Bergen.

"We walk in open our computers and a few class notes and act like normal", Bergen said as they were riding, "and very nonchalantly I will see if I can detect any intrusion into your laptop."

Winslow nodded in silence as they rode along. He was glad he wouldn't have to be doing any of this on his own. "Whenever you have to deal with any sort of conflict or potentially explosive situation it is always best to get a second opinion", he thought to himself.

"I think we should take some photos of the inside of your apartment and examine them later to see if we can find any bugs or spycams that have been placed around." Bergen continued, "How about cutting a hole in the pocket of a shirt, slipping your camera in it and walking around and snapping some photos, you know under the desks, at the nooks and crannies?"

"That sounds like something a ten year old would do", answered Winslow.

"I know I used to do it when I was ten." Bergen replied, "Come on, are you willing to be James Bond with me? If they do have a spycam we don't want them to see us looking around for one. So we secretly take photos."

Winslow was relaxed with the ride and the conversation and felt agreeable and Bergen's logic wasn't entirely indefensible, "Sure why not", Winslow said.

When they got to the apartment they sat down at the desk as planned. Winslow went to the kitchen to get two bottles of water and slice an apple in half. As well as drinking a lot of water, Winslow's policy was that whenever you didn't have a craving for something grossly unhealthy, i.e. sweets and grease, you should always take the opportunity to eat something healthy. He could never motivate himself to cook vegetables at home unless it was in a grilled sandwich, burrito, or pasta he found that he could eat a half of a carrot or apple on a regular basis if he just went into the kitchen with that as a plan. He probably didn't eat the nationally recommended number of fruit and vegetable portions, but with bean burritos on a regular basis, a banana every morning, and the ½ of something every time he went to the kitchen he figured that his diet wasn't that bad. We walked back out into the living room and offered Bergen a bottle of water and a small plate with half an apple. "Courtesy of the house", he said.

Winslow sat down next to Bergen and began looking at some class notes as Bergen fiddled with Winslow's home laptop. Winslow also had inconspicuously got out his digital camera and he was taking a few photos under the desk from various angles. After he got a few photos of the underside of the desk he slipped the camera under his shirt and got up to move about the apartment. He clicked the shutter in his pocket making several turns acting like he was scratching himself and stretching. He also bent over to stretch and pointed that camera at the underside of the other two tables in the room. Finally he sat back down to study with Bergen. The two kept studying with their computers and various class handouts for about an hour. They hardly talked at all.

"Time to head back to classes unfortunately", Winslow stated.

"Yup", Bergen answered, "let's go."

They packed up their papers. Winslow went into the kitchen and flipped on the light over the stove, took one last glance around and they stepped out the door.

CHAPTER SEVEN

After classes Winslow had agreed to meet at a local camera shop where you could download and print photos from your digital camera. Winslow had given Bergen the memory chip from the camera before their separate afternoon class and Bergen had arrived at the camera store before Winslow. When Winslow walked in Bergen was sitting at one of the booths working the mouse and scanning through the various photos that Winslow had taken.

"Nice camera work", said Bergen, as Winslow walked up to him and set his satchel down on the floor. Winslow pulled up a chair and sat down next to him and watched Bergen flip through the tilted images of the various angles of Winslow's apartment.

"It reminds me of the photos I took with my first camera that I got as a Christmas present when I was six", Bergen continued, "It looks like they were taken by a trained monkey or a cat scratching his whiskers on the shutter button. I think we have what we need though.

"Sit down and have a look", Bergen said although Winslow was already sitting down and watching. "So do you want the good news first or the bad news first?"

Winslow replied, "Me? Always the good first. I don't like to take bad news on an empty stomach."

"Ok", said Bergen, "the good news is that we know we are being spied on."

"I assume then that the bad news is contained within the good news?" said Winslow.

"I don't look at it that way", replied Bergen, "We made the right move. They have a track inside your home laptop. They can follow every key stroke if they want. There is an audio bug stuck to the underside of your computer desk, and take a look at this", he zoomed in to a photo that captured a section high on the wall just above a surfing poster Winslow had.

Winslow leaned closer to the monitor. There was no question there was a small circle that had been cut out of the drywall and filled with something that was emitting a slight reflection as if it was made of glass or shiny metal. It obviously had to be a wireless fish eye lens.

Winslow sat back and shook his head, "We are in over our heads. I hope there is no dispute about that now. We had some innocent fun dinking around in the stock scam and insider trading world, but we now have the attention of some people who are a little more serious about it."

Bergen, as predictable, had another view of the situation, "Well I don't know about over our heads. I think we can make a calculated next move and stay a step ahead of these guys. I have a couple of ideas. How about you?"

Winslow answered, "Ideas for what? Our next steps to get deeper into this mess? Are you crazy? We have been tracked out of the anonymity of the cyber world into actual addresses and faces. It's time to close the door on this portal. Good bye, so long. Just a couple of college kids with a little too much free time. We're out of the manipulation market for good. Don't worry about pranks from us anymore."

Bergen answered, the gleam in his eyes growing steadily, "You really don't know how to recognize an opportunity do you?

Winslow felt his frustration grow, at the same time well knowing that Bergen was probably building up to another one of his charismatic arguments to convince him otherwise. Those arguments were the most charming aspect of Bergen's personality, and as much as it sometimes made Winslow's hair stand on edge he couldn't help but enjoy it at the same time.

"You call my apartment being broken into, my computer bugged, and secret mafia microphones and cameras around my apartment an opportunity?", Winslow said.

Bergen laughed suddenly, "Fucking-a I do. You and I have near 1500 SAT's. They have the brains of the better than average criminal. You think we should be scared that they are on to us? They are not on to us. We are on to them."

CHAPTER EIGHT

Gretchen, Winslow and Bergen sat in a booth at the Mexican restaurant munching on chips and salsa and sipping ice water from straws. They had just ordered a beer each and nachos to split. Bergen took a sip from his glass as he continued his hushed conversation about the specifics of how his and Winslow's schemes had led up to finding the bugs in Bergen's apartment, oblivious to Winslow's quiet attempts to shut him up.

Finally Winslow revved up, "Look I don't want her involved in this."

Gretchen countered, "I think I can make my own decisions. Only the boys get to have fun around here?"

Winslow half-heartedly continued his objection, "You want to join our little group of 'geeks gone wild'? I don't think you are the girl I married."

Gretchen replied, "We're not married."

"Oh yeah I forgot, Winslow replied, "I keep thinking we're playing grown up."

Don't play grown up Winslow", Bergen chimed, "Otherwise we can't keep to our chocolate covered version of the story."

"And what is that?" Winslow asked.

Bergen's wit was as quick as usual, "We need to keep our innocence. You know, the innocence of youth verses the corruption and greed of age."

"Is that what we're calling this? Winslow asked again.

Bergen continued, "It has a good ring to it doesn't it? It's almost like we're using our lunch money to bring down Enron executives."

Gretchen had been listening intently and finally joined in, "I've got some lunch money, and I think I know how to take it to the next level. Would you guys let a girl join your tree fort?"

Bergen realized any time he could get Gretchen on his side Winslow would soon topple. He replied with glee. "Alright! The plot thickens. Ensnaring more innocent conspirators. Now I know why he likes you."

The beers had arrived and Winslow took a long swig from his. He relaxed his grip on the on the situation and conceded, "Maybe I'll just leave the room."

Bergen held him back, "Stay. Three devious valedictorian brains are better than two."

"I am serious", Gretchen pushed on, "What if we could hack into the quotes they are getting, so they would be bidding on the numbers we want them to see, instead of the real values?"

Winslow put his chip back in the bowl, "Red alert. Red alert. Can that be done? And if it could would we even want to? "I thought this was just a Weekend at Bernies. You're talking real tech-fraud here."

"Hello, they broke into your apartment and planted mikes and cameras to protect their scheme to rip off investors. Gretchen countered, "What are they going to do, file charges? They might try to blow up your car, but I don't think they are going to come after us in criminal court."

Winslow sighed, "Thanks for the reality check. I feel a whole lot better now."

Gretchen outlined her perspective of the situation, "With the bugs in your apartment we know more about them than they want us to know. We can send them anything we want them to get. Only they won't know they are getting it from us. These days, getting inside someone's computer is like getting inside their brain. It's like we have got our mouse inside their head clicking on what we want them to do. We pull a Pavlov's dog on them. Only we ring the bell after they get the food. So they come to the empty food bowl, we ring the bell, and they go 'Oh, I guess I already ate." Call me sick but I am in. I am so totally in."

Bergen had sat back sipping his beer and relaxing, sucking on the lime that came with the beer and watching the two of them like he might peacefully enjoy watching a football game with no particular investment in the outcome. "Why haven't you married this girl? he said.

Winslow turned to him, "She admits she's sick and you want to marry her?"

Bergen replied, "No. I want you to marry her."

They all realized, despite the seriousness of what they were contemplating, that with the beer and chips and warm lighting of the restaurant the conversation had turned softer and more playful. Winslow finally felt a bit like joking around. "Honey, I think you just got a proposal.", he said to Gretchen.

Gretchen liked to see Winslow in his lighter moods, which she wished happened more often, so she responded with positive reinforcement. "You are having your friends ask me if I want to marry you. I think a note passed in study hall is a little more romantic don't you?"

CHAPTER NINE

Gretchen, Bergen, and Winslow climbed the stairs to the office where Gretchen worked part time for a solo practice securities lawyer. It was about 10pm and the building and stairs were deserted. The office was on the third floor, the elevators were locked out by a code at night, which Gretchen didn't have, but she did have the key to the general access main door of the building and the key to the office where she worked. The lawyer worked by himself, she was his only employee, and his office was one of the smallest and isolated in the building. The door was at the end of the hall and looked like it might have been a mop closet.

"Are your sure he won't mind us sneaking in here after hours to dink around on his computers", Winslow questioned?

"No problem" answered Gretchen, "I do it all the time. I think he is pretty happy to have me around in his lonely little world of conference calls, email negotiations, and stipulations drafted to the court. I get a few freedoms as a result."

Winslow had as inconspicuously as possible gathered as much information about the bugs and taps at his apartment as he could, hopefully without raising the suspicions of the people out there who were watching. He had written down IP addresses on scraps of paper, taken some photos with his cell phone, and downloaded some info onto a flash media card. Once they had discovered the surveillance of his apartment they had been careful to not openly discuss anything at his apartment or to send any emails or make any phone calls with any indication that they had caught on to the surveillance. He had all the information and materials in his shoulder bag and he gave it all to Gretchen once they were in the law office. Gretchen had sifted through the materials and was now logged in on the computer and getting a deeper view of the surveillance, as both boys looked over her shoulder, the blue light of the computer screen and the yellow light of one small desk lamp lighting their faces.

After a few minutes of searching and opening up several screens Gretchen said softly, "Your apartment bugs seem to be sending your secrets to a local street address that doesn't exist. "But some of the spam emails are coming from an IP address registered to a real street address. I think we might know where some of their people work."

Winslow said, "Where?"

Gretchen replied, "In an online trading office right here in our fair city."

Winslow asked, "You're saying the office is a front?"

"No it's a real company", Gretchen clarified, "But I think this stock manipulation has become a side project for them. Doesn't it make sense? How do you get interested in manipulating the stock market? You start out by being a legitimate investor or advisor, and you begin to realize that you can make up your own rules."

Gretchen kept digging deeper and going back and forth between the windows she had opened and finally Winslow said, "I hope you are not thinking of using this information to get us closer to these guys."

Gretchen kept cross checking for a few minutes and gathered her thoughts before replying, "Keep your friends close and your enemies closer. I think I'll go in for a job interview at the company. Nothing like being inside the insiders."

CHAPTER TEN

Gretchen had stayed after hours in the online trading office. There were still a few employees working but things had quieted down enough that she felt she could do some covert investigation without being completely obvious about it, unless someone decided to walk past her cubicle and start looking over her shoulders. Unfortunately that is exactly what happened. Fortunately it was one of the more obviously geeky computer nerd types that didn't have a hugely exciting social life outside of work, and often considered the few chances to interact at the office, especially with the opposite sex, the social highlight of his day. He had seen that Gretchen had stayed late, and was a bit giddy to talk to her in the more personal and intimate setting that of the office that usually warmed up after 6pm. His name was Neil, and despite his slight social clumsiness, the firm had recognized his eye for detail and quick and thorough skills with software and hardware, and he had received some regular but slight promotions in terms of duties and trusts. He had an unofficial role in the computer and account security of the firm, and was often called into the office of the executives to consult on the security of various transactions. Likely in a couple of months he would get an official title and raise that went along with his rapidly developing assistance in the firm in these areas. In short, he was exactly the type of guy that Gretchen could use to get information, and that he had made some fumbling but cute attempts to flirt with her she hadn't been oblivious to.

Neil had walked by her cubicle a couple of times and made a couple of comments like, "Staying late tonight huh?" and "I like it when it is quiet around here like this."

Now he paused at her cubicle and had been talking to her about how things were going on the tennis team, and how she was liking her classes.

He took a moment to look at her computer screen and finally said, "Uhm. I don't think you are supposed to have access to those folders are you?"

Gretchen replied, "Uh, they put me on a special project. I am supposed to look through these for account verification. I guess I should have asked you first."

Neil pondered the sudden switch from enjoying being able to talk to Gretchen informally to having to weigh out his developing position of trust in terms of firm security. He had been casually leaning on her cubicle wall with one hand in his pocket, but now he moved his hand to his face. "Maybe I better make a phone call", he said.

Gretchen felt the heat turning up and realized she better make a move fast. This was definitely a thinking-on-your-feet situation, something she was usually good at, playing tennis required it for one thing, and she quickly weighed her options. She decided to rely on Neil's honesty, realizing that if some people in the firm were up to something shady, his unprecocious integrity would force him to take the high road. His commitment to truth and ethics would outweigh his commitment to the firm. In front of a grand jury Neil is the kind of person who would not hide anything. He would implicate himself if the truth required it. She replied abruptly as he was reaching for the phone, "Wait Neil. Have you noticed anything unusual here? Blanket emails, new stocks being created, that kind of thing?"

Despite his mildly inept social quirkiness Neil was fairly brainy and had moments of making comments that seemed to come from some higher cerebral area than people normally expected from him. He noticed the irony, since Gretchen had only been an administrative assistant at the firm for a month, "Why is a secretary asking me that?" he asked, trying to add a slight edge of humor and humility.

"Maybe I am undercover for the SEC", Gretchen replied.

Neil queried with a slight smile, surprised at his own confidence, "Are you?"

"That's on a need to know basis." Gretchen said, "Do you want to take your chances and wait until the charges are filed and you are walking out of here in handcuffs, or do you want to help me now? I'll put in a good word for you to my supervisors."

Neil pondered the options. There was slight increase in his heartbeat at the fun he was having talking so intimately, and he wished it was easier for him to be more casual and wry in conversations more often. He realized that he didn't want this interaction with Gretchen to end and he realized also that he could explain his assistance to her as part of his loosely defined security duties for the firm if the question ever came up. Finally he answered, "So what do you need exactly?"

CHAPTER ELEVEN

Gretchen, Winslow and Bergen had spent several weeks piecing through the information they had got from Neil's assistance at the securities firm, doing most of the computer work after hours at Gretchen's lawyer office, and were trading ideas on what to do with it. They had begun to realize that they could use the bugged laptop at Winslow's apartment as a Trojan Horse to get virtually inside the accounting records of the OCF, as they were calling the fraud manipulators now (Organized Crime Faction), and download the full identification information of any of the inside investor/partners of the OCF. Part of the problem was that any work on Winslow's home laptop had to be done very in the most surreptitious manner because of its activities were monitored by the bugging chip the OCF had placed. And if they tried to move it, its location would also be tracked. The dilemma was obvious and they discussed solutions.

Winslow lamented, "Once we begin prying into any of their sensitive information the OCF will be on to us and probably breaking into my apartment in minutes."

"No problem", Bergen questioned rhetorically, "What are laptops for if not to go mobile?"

"So what are you proposing, a car chase with us scrambling to get the accounts off the laptop before they surround us?" replied Winslow.

"Sounds fun to me. How about you Gretchen?" Bergen asked.

"Very fun, if they don't catch us that is. And I think we all agreed to keep this fun. So if you have a dynamite plan to keep us a couple of steps ahead of them no matter what, I am along for the ride as always", answered Gretchen.

"Of course I have a dynamite plan" said Bergen, "Do I ever do anything without one?"

"Do you ever do anything with an actual plan, is the more logical question?" replied Winslow.

Bergen as usual had no problem with his character, actions, or motives being challenged, unlike the majority of the population who couldn't help but be governed by their egos, so he rationally enjoyed the ramifications of the challenge for a few moments.

Finally he answered, "You're right Winslow. That's the problem with dynamite plans anyway. They sometimes blow up on you. Anyway we have access to enough information to fry these guys if we want to. I don't have any idea how to get it without getting our fingers burned, but I am sure we will come up with something."

"Well, it sounds like we are all in agreement then" replied Gretchen, pausing for a moment before adding, "But what are we all agreeing to exactly?"

CHAPTER TWELVE

The three had come up with a plan to extract the laptop from Winslow's apartment, hopefully escaping immediate detection by the OCF, and once they had Trojan Horsed themselves into the OCF database to begin searching for what would be the most incriminating and quickly downloadable. They would be on the move while doing this and once the OCF realized that the laptop was gone they would be GPS tracked on a continual basis, and no doubt be chased. The OCF had a lot to hide obviously, they wouldn't know what the college kids were exactly after, but they no doubt had a lot of resources and personnel available to prevent any sensitive information from leaking out of their perimeters. If any did, heads would be on the line. The criminal world was far more ruthless at coming down on employee incompetence and failures than the corporate world.

Bergen sat in the car around the block from Winslow's apartment, just in case there was any surveillance of the building. They didn't know if any more camera's or other surveillance had been added beyond the initial they had discovered, they didn't want to be caught looking around for more stuff, but they had been playing everything very conservatively just in case. The windshield was wet from a slight drizzle that was just tapering off, and the stars could be seen peeking through the cloud cover. Bergen tapped his fingers on the steering wheel and glanced around at the store lights on the boulevard and the few shoppers and partiers stepping out on to the sidewalks to begin enjoying the freshly rain-washed air and streets.

Winslow and Gretchen opened the door to his upstairs apartment and shook off their coats in the hallway. Winslow crept his way in the darkness toward the kitchen to flick on the light above the stove. He had a habit of not preferring ceiling lights, and would much rather just have the used areas of the house lit by area lights; the stove light in the kitchen, and desk lamps or night lights every where else. In the year plus he had lived in this apartment he had never replaced a ceiling bulb since he used them so infrequently. He opened the refrigerator as if it belonged to someone else; unsure of what contents he would find, and was refreshed to see that there was milk.

"Enough for two glasses if you want one", he offered Gretchen.

"No thanks" she answered, "I'm not as much of a calf as you are."

"Well I guess that means I'll have some left for cereal tomorrow." Winslow replied. Despite that they were in a short amount of time likely to be in escape mode from the OCF neither of them was having any problems acting completely natural. They had been in and out of Winslow's apartment often enough knowing they were under surveillance it had become second nature. Still he was surprised at how easy it was especially with the new pressure they were about to put themselves under. "Maybe I should be an actor if I am this cool under the camera," he silently wondered.

Their plan was to try and block the OCF spy camera apartment view enough to swap out his home laptop with his traveling laptop. The wouldn't be able to plug the swapped laptop in to the power strip or make any of the other connections, but with luck they could simply slide the one from his satchel in place of the home one, and in the same movement move the one from the desk into the satchel. They had planned a distraction where Gretchen would start talking about how one of her favorite movie scenes was the one in Pulp Fiction where Uma Thurman as Mia comes into her house and starts the reel to reel recorder and starts singing and dancing to Neil Diamond's "You'll be a Woman soon". While she was dancing around, Winslow would quickly unplug the desk laptop, and after pausing for some more of Gretchen's Uma antics, deftly do the swap leaving the identical traveling laptop in the exact same position as the desk one, which would be slipped inside the traveling satchel.

Gretchen began her distraction, "You know how I envision myself coming home someday?"

"How", Winslow answered.

"Like Uma Thurman coming in to her all white house with John Travolta", she said.

Winslow grinned as he sat down at the desk and began pulling a few textbooks out of his satchel, "Yeah", he said, "I really like that scene. But a reel to reel player? Why would anyone have one of those instead of a CD player?"

"The most practical and efficient isn't always the best guideline to live your life, you know", Gretchen said, "Sometimes you should just toss out efficiency for the sake of pure coolness. You should try it sometimes."

Gretchen moved over to the wall and imitated the movements of Uma switching the reel to reel player. "Girl, dumdumdum", she strummed and imaginary guitar, "You'll be a woman soon, dumdumdum", and began swirling around the apartment in her jacket, raising her arms and seductively swooping down on Winslow shuffling his books and papers on the desk. The plan seemed perfect. The raising and lowering of her arms in a full jacket was almost like a batman cape and easily blocked the view of the spycam. Winslow had unplugged the cords from the laptop, and then done the switch in two quick movements, timed to match her when she swirled next to him.

"I was going to check my emails but screw it", he said in mock anger, "Do we need to know at every minute of the day what other people are thinking?" he asked.

"Right" said Gretchen, "Are we dogs? Do we have to come running every time we hear a whistle?"

"That's the difference between dogs and cats", replied Winslow, "Dogs come running when you call them. Cats take a message and get back to you. I'm more of a cat person myself."

He paused for a moment gathering the view of Gretchen still draping her arms in her long jacket in her Uma Thurma impersonation. "So how do you want your burger?" He queried, "Amos and Andy or Bloody as Hell?"

"I am a cat person too", she replied, "Bloody as hell of course."

Winslow slipped on his coat, turned off the desk lamp but left the stove light in the kitchen on as he always did at night, pulled his satchel over his shoulder, did a full twirl and grabbed Gretchen's hand and began pulling her towards the door.

"So, burgers it is", he said, "But I am going meat free tomorrow. If I don't follow up a burger day with an all fruit and vegetable day I start to feel the cholesterol like a muddy river in my veins. Absolutely yucky."

"Yeah I know", replied Gretchen, "My cholesterol image is like those rivers of mud and debri sweeping up the streets of Sumatra after the tsunami."

Winslow contemplated the image in his head, "It's always good to imprint brutal global images in your brain to keep your perspective and keep focused on the healthy and ethical thing in any situation."

He took one last look around the apartment, glancing to see that the stove burners were off and the coffee pot unplugged although he hadn't touched them at all since they came in, one of his semi-obsessive-compulsive traits, that was none-the-less quite logical. "We're out of here", he said, closing the door.

CHAPTER THIRTEEN

Bergen saw them in his side view mirror as they exited from the alley and started down the sidewalk. He started the car casually and checked all his mirrors for adjustment as they stepped up to the car. Bergen stepped out of the driver's side door and offered Winslow the seat. Gretchen had already got in the back. Bergen gave a wink to Winslow, closed the driver door for him, and then got in the back, wiping off the bit of rainwater that was on his hands from the door handles. Bergen was the only one of them who had a car on campus, and he had let each of them borrow it whenever they wanted it, so it had more or less become the group car over the last couple of months.

He grabbed Gretchen's hand and gave it a squeeze, "Good to see you again sweetheart", he said. She smiled weakly.

Winslow pulled the car away from the curb and began heading up the street. The plan was to stay on small market streets and neighborhoods and keep their speed down. If a chase ensued they didn't want to flag themselves as the car trying to escape. The OCF would likely be able to track them within a block or so fairly quickly, but figuring out which was the kid's getaway car among a bunch of cars all doing the speed limit would be more complicated.

Bergen and Gretchen in the back had the laptop open and were booting it up, their faces lit up eerily by the blue glow of the screen as Winslow picked a random path of turns and streets. To the passerby it looked like two people watching TV in the back being chauffeured around.

Winslow finally said, "How's it going back there? It would be nice if we could get what we need before they get their guys out chasing us. You know, muscled goons with tattoos and weapons, fast cars, weapons, and not paid to listen to our excuses."

"Smooth as silk", Bergen casually underestimated any difficulty they might be having, "I think we are opening the account holder identity file folder now, but they'll probably be encrypted. They didn't want anyone to down load these very fast obviously. Just drive a little faster and make more turns. Space the tracking signals farther apart, assuming they have realized the computer is moving."

Winslow replied, "I hate to tell you but I have never even gotten a traffic ticket before."

Bergen said, "Well you are doing pretty good then. Keep it up Mario amoretti. Minutes are critical."

"How much time do we have?" Winslow asked, glancing back catching Gretchen's eyes and seeing Bergen intently hunched over the screen.

Bergen didn't look up, "How would I know? I guess these guys are serious enough and we've got maybe five minutes tops to get these files and then pass off the computer to some innocent passerby. I thought downloading their account files would only take a few minutes, but I am only at 40% now. We need to keep ahead of them, or hope their tracking is not as good as it probably is."

Kevin was one of the OCF tech specialists and he sat at a desk leaning back lazily in his office chair, glancing periodically at three webcam monitoring screens, occasionally leaning forward to press a few buttons on his keypad and watch the images change on his computer monitor. His ears had become tired from wearing the full headphones so they were sitting to the side of the keyboard. The other tech Nick had pulled his chair fully away from the monitoring station and was drinking a bottled water.

Kevin switched the screen on one of the monitors and looked puzzled. "My signal says the laptop is moving" he finally blurted out.

"What's up Kev", said Nick, sounding entirely unworried, and slowly rolling his chair up to the desk. He looked at the two webcam screens monitoring the apartment, making sure he checked the desk laptop from both angles. "No it isn't. It's still right there", he said, his voice loosing a little of the relax mode he had been in, a slight trickle of adrenalin moving into his veins, and his attention becoming more focused. He set down his water to the side of the desk, and began moving the mouse on the second computer to increase the focus in the dimly lit apartment.

"Its definitely moving", said Kevin again, punching up the GPS monitoring screen, "I've got the laptop at something like ten blocks away from the apartment. Are you sure they didn't change computers. Look closely. Has anything changed?"

Justin brought his face closer to the screen as his hands worked the mouse, "Fuck", he finally said, "The power cord and USB port cords are disconnected. They were connected before right? Either they disconnected them for no reason or they switched computers. Those little weasels. Get Aniston on the radio. We may need some cars rolling now."

Kevin punched in a speed dial on his cell phone and began talking to the party at the other end, "Sir, it looks like they switched laptops. We're tracking the original one now and it is on the road about a mile from the apartment."

He listened to the voice at the other end of the line with a few, "Yes, yes, got it", replies mixed in. The conversation ended, he pressed the 'off' button, and began punching in another speed dial. "We are calling the boys", he said without looking at Justin.

Justin deftly put on a headset with a microphone so that was attached to a closed circuit walkie talkie system and remarked wryly before pressing the radio talk button, "Houston, it looks like we have a problem. Open the communication lines. Launch the emergency pod and let's get mobilized."

The OCF had two drivers who were contracted to be mostly mobile at all times. Usually they were used for mundane equipment or message pick up and delivery, sometimes as chauffeurs, but if anything required something more devious or criminal they were called on to be the heavies and they were paid in relation to the risk they assumed. Kevin and Justin were now in communication with them. They had the aliases of T1 and T2 for any radio or cellphone communication, and it was common knowledge among the OCF that the T designation originated from the "Terminator" movies.

Justin spoke into the headset, giving directions to one of the drivers, "T1 come in. Are you mobile? We need to follow a Labrador Retriever on the loose. Can you confirm your location. I have the Labrador at the 3000 block of Wilshire, heading south." 'Labrador Retriever' was the code for the laptop in Winslow's apartment. As well as the laptop having a code, so did Bergen, Winslow, and Gretchen. The OCF often used dog or cat breeds as a code for anything that needed to be kept cryptic in communications; the first letter of the breed usually matching the first letter of the item or person that was discussed. Bergen was 'Basenji', Winslow was 'Whippet', and Gretchen was "German Shepherd". As a result the members of the OCF had become somewhat of an expert on dog and cat breeds.

The driver replied back, "Copy, I am about two miles away, moving now. Is there a vehicle description?"

Justin answered, "Negative, all we have is the location of the Lab. I would look for a car with any of the other dogs in it."

T1 had a file with the surveillance photos of Bergen, Winslow, and Gretchen. He glanced at it to refresh his memory and then answered, "Copy, keep me updated on the location. T1 out."

Justin spoke again, "T2, did you copy, can you engage also?"

T2 replied, "Copy, I'll be there in two."

Winslow kept driving as Bergen and Gretchen worked at the computer in the back. He asked. "Do you think they are closing on us? Can we ditch that computer yet? How's my driving?"

"Your driving is great", replied Bergen, "In fact when this is all over I am calling the 1-800 number to give you a kudo."

He kept focus on the laptop screen for a few moments and then added, "But first I have another idea to throw them off the track. Gretchen, mind if I borrow your GPS?"

Winslow glanced in the rear view mirror with a perplexed look, "Why are we lost?"

"No, we are trying to get lost", Bergen answered and then continued, "Gretchen, do you have a USB cable with you?"

Gretchen perked up, "I never leave home without one. I am way ahead of you. You want me to send them a fake GPS location. How do you feel about Reno?"

Bergen chuckled, "No, we don't want them to think we've jammed their tracking. We just need them to take a wrong turn or two. It won't buy us much time, but we don't need much. I am at 60% copied now. Dial in a location."

Gretchen worked the GPS as she listened to Bergen's explanation, "Got it. The GPS will say we are turning right at the next street. That means we go left."

Winslow listened to the team in the backseat and fondly shook his head, "Wow, you guys are really fun. Most the people I drive for just want a ride to the concert or the airport. OK, left it is."

Justin and Kevin looked at there large monitor which had a GPS map on screen. They watched the flashing orange blip that indicated the location of the laptop. They were now communicating the exact turns and streets that the laptop was at as it casually winded its way through residential and minor shopping district streets. Justin had an open radio channel with

T1 and T2 and was directing them as they were closing in on the kids, although since they didn't have a vehicle description they would have to get close enough to identify the kids in the car before they boxed them in.

The plan was to just get the laptop and then get out of there before they attracted the interest of any law enforcement. T1's plan was to walk up to the car with a gun under his coat and say, "Open the door and hand me the computer or I will shoot my way in. All we want is the computer. Now." He figured the kids would not be able to dispute the obvious logic of saving their own skins, since likely this whole event was at least partially just a playful diversion from their studies that had taken a wrong turn, and if they hadn't realized that yet, they were about to.

Justin spoke into his headset, "T1 and T2 location and status. The Lab just turned south on Mesa. Have you got a visual, over?"

Both T1 and T2 had their radios on open communication in hands free mode so they could just speak as if they were all having a conversation. Justin had suggested and set up the radio option a number of months ago, rather than cell phones, and had trained T1 and T2 in their use, just for this type of scenario, and he felt a bit of pride in seeing the system working flawlessly in action. "Shut up and drive", was one of Justin's mottos, and he made a habit of unless absolutely necessary never talking on a cellphone while driving, and he considered the concept of texting while driving even more ridiculous.

"South on Mesa, South on Mesa" he repeated, "Have you guys got them, over?"

T1 replied, "Making the turn now. Should be just a few seconds."

T2 replied also, "Coming in from the south, I should get a visual, I see a car coming, I think I've got them."

T2 slammed on his brakes before having a head on collision with the vehicle that had been coming down Mesa from the north. As he got out of the driver's side door he took one step toward the other car before his face dropped in disappointment. T1 was getting out of the other car and they looked at each other with an instant realization of what had just happened. The kids had proved again that they were not to be underestimated. They had jammed the tracking. They may have been following a legitimate signal for most of the chase, but the kids had pulled some techno trick to spin them in the wrong direction at the last moment.

T1 and T2 looked at each other for a moment and through up their hands in disappointment. They had followed instructions so they weren't worried that they would take the heat for this, so they each grinned at each other slightly. "Well", T1 said, as he walked back to his car and stuck his head in the window so he would be back on radio communication with Justin.

"T1 here, along with T2 on Mesa", he stated, "Looks like the dog has vanished. No visual, nothing. Awaiting further instructions."

CHAPTER FOURTEEN

"Got it", said Bergen, "Download complete, and I think this enough information to really make the OCF squirm, at least I think they'd be willing to buy you a new laptop or two for it Winslow. Mind if we find someone who wouldn't question a gift computer from a passing car?"

Winslow nodded, "No problem, I sort of expected that would be the plan. Let's get rid of it before they debug the bogus GPS signal and start chasing us again. Any kind of trailer trash will do. Homeless person, street goths. Any ideas, keep your eyes open"

The kids saw a group of post-teen skateboarders doing rails on the curb and pulled up to them. Gretchen leaned her head out the window, "Hey uh, anyone need a laptop? We're going to the store to get new ones with our rebate checks."

The skateboarders approached the car. One of them came up to Gretchen and said, "Rebate checks? Are they still giving those out? Sounds like a made up story to me."

Gretchen replied, "Oh look, a cynical skateboarder. Distrusting of society in general. How novel. You want a free computer or not homeboy?"

The skateboarder looked at her intently for a few seconds then answered, "Sure girlfriend we'll take it. Why don't you leave your handsome college boyfriends in the car and come party with us street creeps for a while, or do we only get the computer?"

"This is a hardware deal only", replied Gretchen, "No software included". She held the laptop out the window and the skateboarder stepped up and took it.

"In the meantime, why don't you guys stop surfing on concrete and go catch some real waves", Gretchen said as the skateboarders stepped away from the car, "I never understand the appeal of surfing concrete."

"Good point", said the skateboarder, "Maybe we'll trade the laptop for a surfboard. Anyway have fun with your rebates and thanks for mingling with the street creeps for a few minutes. We always enjoy it when you upper middle income types stop by to give us the respect we don't deserve. Adios."

"Our pleasure", Gretchen winked at them as Winslow pulled the car away from the curb.

"I am in the mood for some tennis", said Winslow, "Too much stress without any aerobic stress relief gets me edgy. I'm running on all adrenaline and no serotonin. Let's let Bergen off somewhere with the disk, and hit the tennis court to clear our heads so we can plan our next move. I am sure that you guys are planning a next move."

Bergen agreed, "Right I'll take the disk and get lost. You guys make the call to the OCF and see if they want to negotiate."

"Definitely sounds good to me", said Gretchen, "I'm up for the tennis court also. Let's loosen up for a bit while they simmer in uncertainty. The more they sweat the more negotiating leverage we have."

Winslow drove for a few more minutes more along the gentrified retail boulevard and finally pulled over next to a coffee shop to let Bergen out.

"Thanks for letting us borrow your car", said Winslow.

"No problem", said Bergen, "I only need a piece of it anyway, so you guys can have the other pieces. We are students after all. Catch up with you guys later."

Winslow and Gretchen were in shorts and tee-shirts and hitting tennis balls in the indoor tennis bubble of the local private tennis club. Neither Gretchen nor Winslow were formally members of the club, but Gretchen's parents were, and the club had a contract arrangement with the college that the women's tennis team could use the indoor bubble any available evenings. Also if the weather wasn't suitable for outdoor matches on match days, the club contract permitted the women's tennis matches to be held in the bubble. The club members generally didn't mind the loss of court time, since many of them enjoyed the chance to watch the college team play, and many were alumni of the college and supporters of the academic and athletic programs.

They had played two sets, almost even, and were now sitting on the bench wiping sweat and drinking water from the bottles they had bought from the vending machine at the entrance of the bubble. Usually they brought their own water bottles that they just kept re-using, as much for the cost as for the complete environmental impracticality of buying bottled water, but today was a splurge day, and a little treat like bottled water from a vending machine was worth its weight in just winding down with a little luxury.

Gretchen wiped her hands on a towel and pulled her cellphone out of a pocket in her tennis bag. She had an after hours phone number she had got from the securities firm that she figured if it wasn't a direct line to someone in the OCF at least it would put her in touch with someone who would know how to contact them. She hadn't called the number yet, no point in disclosing any more of what you know than is absolutely necessary. She figured that she would be calling this number eventually, and the time was now. They didn't have the downloaded disk with them, so if the OCF wanted to simply track them and capture them, Winslow and Gretchen had nothing to offer. They didn't even know where Bergen was at this point. Thus she figured they had leverage and safety, and she was able to put some of her nervousness aside as she made the call.

As the other party picked up, Gretchen said, "Did you find us yet?"

"Find who, who is this?" the party answered.

"Oh a couple of kids from the university with some information we probably shouldn't have", she said, "Did I call a wrong number?"

"Just a moment", the party answered.

She heard a bit of conversation in the background and then the phone went dead.

"They hung up", she said to Winslow, "What does that tell you?"

"That I think you had the right number", he replied. "I bet they are talking about us right now, fondly I hope, but I wouldn't cross my fingers."

They both anticipated a call back, probably within the half an hour, once their cellphone number had been given to the correct party, and the OCF had organized their thoughts for how to approach the situation. Clearly the OCF had to be worried about whatever files had been downloaded, they had underestimated the skills of the college kids up until now, and their next move had to be carefully planned out. The college kids had outwitted the lower levels of the OCF management and had thus earned the right to deal directly with the top of the organization, and he was being contacted now to decide how to move next.

Winslow started putting his racket and towel in his tennis bag and slipped on his light tennis windbreaker. "Now what I think we need to fully complete the wind-down process is some alcohol. I picture an appetizer and a couple of glasses of red wine at someplace fancy, how does that sound to you?" he asked Gretchen

CHAPTER FIFTEEN

Winslow and Gretchen had showered at the club and were about halfway through their first glasses of wine and a couple of plates of appetizers. As a rule Winslow was frugal about everything, but to his credit he realized the importance of identifying the time to splurge and enjoy life. You didn't need to live beyond your means on a daily basis to feel like the good life was passing you by, rather if you picked a few choice occasions to sample from the expensive side of the menu, figuratively speaking, you appreciated it more. This was definitely one of those moments and Winslow was savoring the wine, appetizers, and relaxation to the fullest. For all practical purposes this indulgence would effectively be on the tab of the OCF if the information the kids had on the disk was likely as valuable as they thought it was.

Winslow felt the relaxation of the couple of sets of tennis, the hot shower, the wine, food and dim lighting engulfing him warmly. He cherished that feeling of pushing your self hard, especially on the tennis court, and then following that up by allowing the parasympathetic nervous system to completely take over and flood your system with the hormones of relaxation. He smiled at Gretchen, feeling no need to speak, as they both savored the moment. They were expecting a phone call at any time, and finally Gretchen's cell phone rang.

Gretchen answered, "Hello?"

"Hello back", the voice answered, "I am returning a call. I just want to make sure I am speaking to the party I am speaking to, if you don't mind the 'Laugh In' joke."

"Not at all", answered Gretchen, "Contrary to popular belief, we do have a sense of humor. I personally don't trust anyone without one."

"I can respect that", the voice on the other end answered, "And as for whether or not your sense of humor has been lost on anyone here, it hasn't been lost on me. I especially like the Lords of Dogtown touch."

"We like simple non-polluting transportation you can carry in your backpack and empty swimming pools", answered Gretchen.

"So does everyone at some point, but we all grow up eventually", the voice answered, "A fun bunch of skaters indeed, although I think them demanding $1000 for a used laptop bought on a street corner was a little harsh, but the leader had a little more savvy than his social status may have indicated. I think he figured out he was holding something of value to someone. I predict great things for him."

"I do also", replied Gretchen, "There is a random distribution of brain power in society at any point in time. The smart ones take a while to be recognized by the masses, if ever, so a percentage of the time important decisions are being made by people who should barely be trusted to fill a grocery list."

Gretchen was glad that the voice at the other end of the line was so conversational. She felt glad to be dealing with someone with a brain, a sense of reason, and the likelihood of coming to a reasonable compromise without the inefficiency of any more car chases or gang style operations. The voice had sounded familiar from the first moment she heard it, and suddenly she placed it. It had to be Professor Sanford, and she was about to blurt it out whey she realized that it would be better to not say his name out-loud; it would give the kids more leverage if the OCF knew they could at least trust the kids to not be petty.

After processing the advantages of not speaking Sanford's name in case it may be recorded, she said finally, "Your voice sounds familiar. Maybe we know each other."

"Maybe we do", answered the voice, "In any event I think we should get to know each other better. How does the rest of the evening look for you?"

"Tired", replied Gretchen. Let me talk to my associates and we'll do breakfast in the morning. How does that sound?"

"I do my best work at breakfast", replied the voice. "Did you know that dreams are a process your brain goes through to sort out and reassemble the thoughts and events of the day?"

"Will that be on the exam?" asked Gretchen. The comment on brain process was the type that someone with a natural inclination to teach would make, and she was even more sure now that she was talking to Sanford. His next statement confirmed it.

"It will be important", the voice answered. "Anyway, add coffee to the effects of sleep and dreams sweeping the dust from your brain and putting everything back on the shelf and you have your peak clarity at the beginning of the day. Never make any important decisions late in the day. Draft an email but don't send it. Get up in the morning, have your coffee and then look at it again. You will always see something you missed or decide to delete something stupid. Anyway breakfast it is. I think we have each other's numbers."

Gretchen looked at Winslow across the table. "You want to take a break from this and meet my new friend in the morning?" she asked, letting her voice be audible into the cell phone. Winslow nodded.

"We'll talk tomorrow", she said into the cell phone, "Adios".

"Hasta manana", the voice replied and then the line went dead.

CHAPTER SIXTEEN

In contrast to the organized central offices of the securities fraud investigation unit Jacobson normally holed himself up in sleazy motel rooms with his computer, two cell phones, and handful of mobile surveillance equipment that he had become an expert with during his short term stint as a private investigator. He had used the part time income from that to put him through a two year crime program at the local community college. The classes were easy for him, and the college had an effective job placement program that had quickly got him an interview for a low end job with the federal government. His supervisor with the feds had overlooked Jacobson's unpolished demeanor in favor of his grades and private investigation experience and had hired him unofficially on the spot. He had to continue the rest of the interviews and formally document that Jacobson was the best qualified candidate but for all practical purposes the decision was made at the interview in a manner of minutes.

His supervisor was old school and he didn't get snowed easily by groomed college hot shots who were just looking at the entry level position as a quick stepping stone to pass over anyone in their way. His supervisor also knew that the department had a need for inconspicuous and more committed than ambitious operatives for somewhat undercover fraud investigations, and Jacobson fit the profile perfectly. Jacobson also didn't demand much in the way of perks and was content to find the cheapest accommodations possible to get down to doing what he did best; his job, in any format that might take. Whenever he was given an assignment he listened carefully, took notes, and had no ego whatsoever in terms of being asked to do something he didn't want. His supervisor had predicted those character aspects when he met Jacobson and wasn't surprised when his prediction proved accurate. It wasn't long before Jacobson was given just basic instructions and relied upon to make his own judgment based upon his street sense and dedication. He didn't require nearly as much direction and supervision as people in the department making twice what he was making and unlike many others in the public sector his work ethic and quality would easily pass scrutiny of an outside commission.

Jacobson had been assigned to this stock scam case for about 6 months. The organized crime group he was investigating was smart, careful, well armed with the latest technology, and had lawyers that could easily chew up and spit out any federal case that wasn't put together with absolute precision. Jacobson knew that he wouldn't be able to get them for anything major; they were too smart for that, but with luck he may be able to get them into court for something minor that would at least stop them for a while or adopt methods that were quite so ruthless. It was a game of cat and mouse, and everyone knew it. Ironically enough he had come up with OCG as the term for the organized crime group.

Monitoring the OCG cell phone and computer communications had been spotty, but Jacobson had been able discover some of the locations they operated out of, and was able to provide enough information to his central command to be able to monitor their radio communications. He had heard the car chase, had been able to follow Gretchen and Winslow to the tennis club and now to the restaurant. He had taken up a booth opposite them and a few tables down and had his concealed sound amplifying unidirectional microphone pointed at them as they had the cell phone conversation with Sanford.

He had planted a lo-jack tracking bug on their car so he was confident he would be able to follow them to their meeting in the morning.

CHAPTER SEVENTEEN

Gretchen, Winslow and Bergen had set up the meeting with the voice at the other end of the line, whom they all agreed with Gretchen's interpretation that it was likely Sanford. They picked a chain diner instead of one of their normal student breakfast, muffin, and coffee restaurants. A meeting between students and some either completely wall street types or mafia types or some blend of the two would probably stand out at the student cafes. At a national chain diner anything could go down and likely not look out of place. The three students grabbed a booth and started looking over the menus.

"Do you think they'll buy us breakfast?", asked Bergen.

The café had cleared out from the breakfast rush when a figure appeared silhouetted by the bright low morning light in the doorway.

"My guess is that is our guy", said Gretchen, "lit up like an epiphany. Do we need any more of a sign that this whole episode is going to come crashing down on us in the next 60 seconds with all secrets and mysteries revealed?"

"If that guy tells us if we can get out now or go for a ride in his car to some warehouse for further clarification, I am taking option #1", chimed Winslow.

The figure approached; they didn't recognize him.

"Well, so it is 'team clueless' as we all call you back at the office", the voice said as he removed his sunglasses and came closer. "Good job you guys, quite impressive for a three college kids with nothing more than high SAT scores."

"I assume you are going to let us in on the secret, including who you are", inquired Bergen.

"Of course", the man said, "Jacobson, Securities and Trade Commission. Can I buy you breakfast? I think you have probably earned it." Jacobsen pulled up a loose chair to their booth, "Mind if I sit?"

"Do we have a choice?" said Gretchen.

"Of course", said Jacobsen, "I am here to offer you a choice. We are on the border of criminal stock practices and the possibility of immunity for testimony, that kind of thing, but we prefer to keep it more informal. Friendly and cooperative; recognizing your blind innocence and youth. That kind of thing. Any problem so far?"

Winslow raised his hand sheepishly, "Not here your honor".

"I didn't think so", said Jacobsen. "You should know that we have been monitoring you, and your excellent but naïve efforts at getting in over your head brought us to the group we have been trying to get at for the last year. We have a few members in custody, and indictments are being drafted as we speak. All things considered, we got our guy, and we are willing to look the other way from your foray into the manipulation market, assuming you are all willing to walk out of this café and go back to doing your homework and graduating without ever crossing that line again."

The three looked at each other, quickly pondering the entire affair, the success, the money, the fun and the fear. An agreement was reached without words.

"We are willing to cut our losses, well winnings actually", said Winslow, "I have a class in an hour, and I don't really have the time to be messing with any of this high stakes skullduggery any more. I have had my fun."

"Smart kid", said Jacobsen, "Now how about breakfast? Nothing like a car chase and stake-outs to get up your appetite."

www.ingramcontent.com/pod-product-compliance
Lightning Source LLC
Chambersburg PA
CBHW021024180526
45163CB00005B/2109